SHADES

OF

AUTUMN

BY

ALICE MOHLER

ISBN# 1-56411-335-3
YBBG# 0331

Published in the U. S. A.
By
CONQUERING BOOKS, L.L.C.
210 East Arrowhead Drive #1
Charlotte, N. C. 28213
(704) 509-2226
www.conqueringbooks.com

October in the hills of Virginia, a time when the green has turned to gold and the wind carries that woodsy smell from some brush fire. The clouds are high, the sky hazy, all that was new is now old and almost gone for yet another season. White tail deer graze openly in the fields, for the guns of the hunters are still quiet. Farmers are busy getting in their last harvest. The women, busy canning and freezing for soon the snows will come. Its then quietness comes to the hills. Lazy smoke drifting from chimneys, and occasional barking of some dog out chasing game. At night, when the cold winds are howling around the corners, ice forming on the windowpanes. The kids are tucked into their feather beds with the quilts piled high.   Mom and dad sitting beside the fireplace, him, strumming the guitar and mom softly singing old country and western ballads. All seems right with your world and you truly feel that right now is all there is, so it is in the days of our youth.

All too soon, those days of believing in magic fade. There comes this time of needing to be validated but, quickly learning if others approve, you must be good and if they don't, you must be really bad. Some how you grow up, in years anyway, but leaving you so insecure. You struggle all your life to figure out how come your such a bad person, what did you do wrong and when. Approval is all you want but it never comes. Although your years are numbered as many, that five year old little girl from those October days is still hiding just out of sight.

Only when you become one within yourself do you truly grow up, or at least have a chance at life. You begin to know that life just is, and that in life, everything and everyone is perfect and as it all should be. You finally realize it's the perspective of each individual that causes the pain and then trying to impose their will on you. Each of us must find our own truth about what's right or wrong for them. We gage this by that deep feeling inside that's always there to direct our path. Only by listening to our inner self do we find the strength, courage, and the peace to truly go forth and fulfill our destiny, to bloom, to become that woman/child who can look back on those October days and believe in the magic of life once again.

Table Of Contents

<u>*Aposticope To Myself*</u>

Alone am I, once again
the golden sun, now just a glow
today is gone, merely a glimmer
Another page of life now stilled
There are smiles for things
Well done.
Tender thoughts
for loves now scattered
Alone am I, at setting sun.
But within my heart
I hold all that matters.

<u>It's Not The Wind</u>

It's full of whispers
The wind at night
Full of sighs
of things undone
The lost words
the empty dreams
Scream on the wind
like things unseen
But, we know it's not the wind
That brings the haunts alive
It's all the things, we failed to do
In our struggle to survive.

<u>Life's Night</u>

Quiet and peaceful
As most havens are.
Foreign and distant
As new places seem.
Memories like clouds
    that block out the sun
Come in the night, and,
    tear out the dreams
And I, tired and alone
    reach for a time
When darkness will go
    waiting not knowing
Yet knowing inside
Daylight nor darkness
I, from memories can't hide
Lost somewhere between
    today and the past
Knowing these moments
    Can't, won't last.

<u>Life Is For Sharing</u>

When you're tired
And, the world closes in.
Put away your fears
Know you can win
Smile - tho you're blue
let your heart roam free
Think about others
try and you'll see.
Life does get easier
time will have wings
And you, you get this feeling
that only sharing brings

<u>Leaving the Past</u>

Healing the past
with hopes for tomorrow
Dreaming of happiness
forgetting the sorrow
Sadness can drown
the most beautiful dreams
Leaving us empty
living on schemes
Time is not gentle
to those who don't live
Life is but wasted
until you can give

Doubts – Removed

I fashioned for myself
a gown of blackest black
There was no crown upon my head
nor wings upon my back
My soul full of dread
As I climbed that spiral case
To knock upon Heaven's door
And not find for me a place
The door opened wide
I looked on My Father's face
He held out his arms for me
'Welcome Home my child.'
I looked down and to my surprise
My gown had changed to white
There were jewels upon my head
My Soul, filled with Light.

<u>No Time for Tears</u>

There was no time for tears
yet the sadness marched in
Leaving me tossed
Lost on the wind
Days, full of motion
Nights, free of pain
But, stealing like a thief at night
It all came back again
There is no happy medium
not one within my view
So may I stay a little while
And draw some strength from you

Touchings

The warmth of the sun
The cool of the night
feelings, like breezes
always aflight
Touches so gentle
feelings so deep
Moments that stay
Forever - today

<u>Boundaries</u>

Walls are two fold
as most things are
Holding in the warmth
keeping out the cold
Walls are but Boundaries
for things yet and not
Linked by ideas
Some real and some not

<u>My Life At A Moment</u>

My life came to a close today
But, I couldn't shut the door.
Losing a fight
for a distant dream
Leaving my Soul weary and sore
Tears fell as rain
in a raging storm
I felt I could go on no more
no more

<u>Drawing In</u>

Candles white –
Candles bright –
Glowing in the night
Drawing home
Some lonely one
Lost out in the night

<u>Being Alone</u>

Alone, with loneliness all around
Everything within
Crying - Can't you hear
Full of tears that can't be shed
Sounds that keep on sounding
They overpower your head
Heart, that keeps on beating
So, to stifle all your fears
Time does not pass easy
The Price - Just pain and tears

Lost - Alone
Pain - raging inside
Looking and searching
For things you can't find
Smiles in the morning
Touches at night
In between these
Contentment - Life

<u>The Clock</u>

A measurer of time
without, any regrets.
No thoughts, no feelings
It measures, lets pass
Then simply, forgets
It's a true marvel
The clock on the shelf
Ticking and chiming
Day-in and day-out
Passing the moments
Like dew on the grass
Real for now
But, does not last

<u>Death</u>

We've walked together so many times
Along the rails of time
You on one side, I the other
Together, yet so
I hold the vigilance
You are the goal
of one, between us lay
So dear death, each time we meet.
On that sweet bed of laurel
Tread easy, least my soul might break
Before it meets God's goal

<u>Once Again Death</u>

So, dear death, we'll meet again
I feel you very near
Your chill has reached the threshold
of one, they hold so dear.
God gives us life
You take away
So I must surmise the rest.
You must be the hand of God
Reaping his very best.

Time of Solace

Jesus came to visit today
He stayed a little while
I smiled and talked
He gave me strength
To go another mile

<u>You Are A Blessing</u>

He said, 'You're not beautiful
Just to look at you
But, your eyes reflect the gentleness
that glows from within
Your smile is like the morning sun
Your touch a soothing breeze
among my many blessings.
I count you as one of these.
You can't help me pass away
Just please sit quietly by my side.
I'm thankful for your friendship
the strength that you provide
As this life fades
And my new one, full of peace.
Holds me ever in its arms
I'll always recall your face.'

Ode to Rt. 151

Winding through the valley
Like a ribbon gone astray
Only touching just the edges
Where people choose to stay
Glaring when the sun beats down
with rain it's shiny black
Barren when it's colder
But, it can always take you back
Back home where times were easy
A place where dreams came true
When life was just a promise
When all your world was new.
Now, from my view on this hill
I suddenly realize
It never really stops at all
It merely passes by.

<u>Faded Love</u>

Love flows easy
on a two way street
Time seems to stand still
each time we meet
Hearts that are peaceful
our minds warm and true
Just knowing each other
makes the whole world new
Life remains gentle
having our dreams
Sharing some moments
with quietness between
When love is over
with only memories left
Just smile and feel great
for the love we have felt
My mountains I will leave behind
As a new life beckons
Meadows filled with buttercups

Waters cool and blue
I look across the valley
That was home when I was young.
Seeing only sad reminders
of song that have been sung

Is this life
Walls, silence all around
Will the grave be kinder
Will it muffle my sounds
Rest - oh blessed peace
As time marches on, unseen
My world - but a memory
My life - just a dream

<u>*Portrait of a Shadow*</u>

At times there comes a sadness
Stealing in without a noise
Rising like the blacken clouds
Just before a storm
There is no need to feel this way.
Least, my head reasons so
But, it's my heart that feels the rains
As the storms come and go

There are so many pictures
within my head tonight
I try to hold one image
Quickly it fades from sight
There is no time but now
Yet, ghost run in and out
They bring a fleeting glimpse
of loss, of pain, of death
The loss of old dear friends
of pain that never ends

of death and his chariot black
and I, never going back
So, come in if you like
Just leave a piece of you.
When tomorrow comes
I will cove it with gold

Winter's Wind

Spring was at our doorstep
Days of winter flown
When from the west
the snow appeared
Blinding our every move
It was the wind
that harmed us most
that relentless, cold chill
It froze the budding Easter flowers
Spring just collapsed around our shells
We strive to find the gentleness
We know life does hold
Only to find
when we get near
it's changed
by the blowing cold

<u>Love Revisited</u>

I touched your hand
I see your face
I recalled the parting words
If I could say I love you –
I would do that today
If I could say forever
that would happen too –
But, life is and lives are.
Of the past, we've made
If we could be as we were –
No other lives but ours –
We would mold tight our lonely hearts
And, all the world be ours.

Good-Night Sweet Lady

Your body lays wasted now
You out grew the need of it
Before your soul departed
You so enjoyed life, didn't you
You had such a flair
An eye for beauty.
A compassionate heart
A gently smile
I just wanted to thank you
For sharing a time with me
I shall always remember.
Good-night my sweet lady.

Sun coming up
Pink fingers across the sky
Pushing away the darkness
Another day, the cost can I buy
The pain stayed so close
Crying in the night
Will this be the day
I finally lose the fight

On Passing Away

It's always sad
when a life is ending
And, the angels call
picking up and putting away
Love for her alone
But, God waits on the other side
A veil that is so thin
He'll pick her up, leave the pain
Then she'll be new again

A warm sunny day
A carefree drive
Life is much easier
With you by my side
Feeling so deep
to you, they do flow
And yours to me
As onward we go
A warmness so gentle
It hurts to think
The idea of losing
Yet, Hearts, easy break

A stately tree whose life began
Quite sometime ago.
It gives us shade
and fresh clean air
It's home to those
who run and fly
It's seen the seasons
come and go
It's roots run deep - deep below
The masses pass, all around
It views them like
a child, a clown

Accepting

These lonely hours come and go
they wave to me in passing
The ticking of their measure
Mocks me like a passion
The pain comes and cuts me quick
it leaves no room for reason.
Within this space, marked by timer
I realize –
this is my season

<u>Poems Are but Patches</u>

My poems are but patches
taken from my life in passing
Hoping to give to another
Needed insight - that is lasting
When my life is over.
When all the pieces fit
Smile and say to another
'Some Life, wasn't it.'

My Dad (Memories)

You came creeping in today
All though my head was full
You came deep from within
Memories were old, yet from the start
they lingered long
They tore my mind
that they could feel so new.
I did not sing nor shed a tear
just sadly recalled, it's been many a year.
Since I've looked upon your face
felt your kiss, your warm embrace
You're gone, but it seems like at your will.
At the strangest times I remember still.

Skies rumble
      Rain falls
Leaves tremble
      Life continues.